The Boat Rocker

The Boat Rocker

A Poetry of Life

Michael Mann

iUniverse, Inc.
New York Lincoln Shanghai

The Boat Rocker
A Poetry of Life

Copyright © 2004 by Michael S. Pendergast III

iUniverse books may be ordered through booksellers or by contacting:

iUniverse
2021 Pine Lake Road, Suite 100
Lincoln, NE 68512
www.iuniverse.com
1-800-Authors (1-800-288-4677)

ISBN: 0-595-33970-0 (pbk)
ISBN: 0-595-67044-X (cloth)

Printed in the United States of America

To the five great loves in my life whose worth has commanded my respect and love;
To those five great loves in my life who I have chosen to give my love and respect.
But most especially,
To my first Love, to whom all glory is due,
And to my last love, ma Coeur, without whom
These poems could and would not have been written.

Contents

Introduction

This is a book of poetry—but it is also a book of philosophy, life's philosophy. It has been said that philosophy begins in awe and wonder, and since that is true, this book is a book of poetry, not academic prose in which awe and wonder are all to often dried out and lifeless, desiccated, and turned to dust to be blown into insubstantial wisps of nothingness. This is a book of poetry filled with life's substance. And if the poems are not always perfect or complete, what of it?—Our lives are not perfect and complete. If a poem's rhyme or meter falters here and there, what of it?—Our way in life is sometimes out of tune, and occasionally faltering too. Yet our persistence, our determination to live and walk with Life must not falter. And to do that, our awe and wonder must not falter either, for if we do not push on, life itself will succumb and be blown into insubstantial wisps of nothingness. We must have confidence and belief and we must act—for if we do not act or believe or have confidence in life and ourselves and our Creator, we do not live, and a life unlived is not a life at all.

This is a book of poetry—but it is also a book of philosophy, my philosophy. It has been said that a man's philosophy is his autobiography, and since that is true, this book is my autobiography, my life. It is filled with my blood and sweat and tears. It is filled with my dreams and hopes and fears. This is a book filled with a record of things attempted, things done, some with a measure of success and others with only abject failure—but with things acted upon, believed in, and at least striven for with confidence, and that confidence has been rewarded with a life lived; with a life which is far greater than mere existence and survival. It is a record of a life lived, for a life unlived is not a life at all.

Marquette University
25 November 2004

Come, Muirnin

I hope that in far decades, dear,
That you will sometime be,
The sweet but still shy maiden,
Who now craves a touch from me:

A bounteous heart still filled with love,
Whose lips still shyly smile,
Who can't believe she's found her love,
Yet knows it all the while.

Who can't believe her fortune,
Who trembles at the thought,
Come, muirnin, give your heart away,
You know that's as it ought.

Come, muirnin, place your hand in mine,
Give me your trembling heart.
And I will hold it in my hands,
And protect it as I ought.

And in the decades long from now,
I will protect it still,
For it will be my treasure,
But you'll be wherein I dwell.

Come, muirnin, give your heart to me,
There's naught for you to fear,

For I will give this back to you,
Every day of every year:

My heart that trembles at the thought,
Of finding its own true self,
And can't believe its fortune,
Yet knows to what it's left:

In pleasure's times and suffering's times,
We two'll live thru 'ere that comes,
Sustained by the beat of a single heart,
Of two…who will be one.

Michael Mann

For Love of a Young Lass

One day as I lay upon my bed,
My pillow 'neath my weary head,
Seeking a brief respite from toil,
I had a waking dream:

I lay upon another bed,
The pillows prop'd behind me…
So that I lay and yet I sat,
My lover's form beside me.

She snuggled inside the crook of my arm,
And quietly lay, close and warm,
Dressed in a gown of virginal white,
A vision of delight.

One cup was pulled down from her breast,
And on it nuzzled in peaceful rest,
Mouth sucking on a small pink rose,
The fruit of our two's love.

And as I stroked my true love's hair,
She in turn stroked our child's head there,
A lass who slurped quite noisily,
A breast I happily shared.

Then suddenly the dream was gone,
And it was I, now rested and warm,
No longer weary, no longer tired,
For I'd seen the dream to come.

Understanding

Have the strength, my own true love,
    to be as weak as I,
To place yourself into the hands
    of the Spirit in the sky.
Please be poor in spirit
    and give yourself to Him today,
For He'll return your soul to you,
    more yourself in every way.

Have the strength, my own true love,
    to dismiss your pride and fear,
For no guarantees can e'er be given,
    that these two would ever hear.
And no guarantee is strong enough,
    not even for true love,
But love's a glimpse of heaven, dear,
    and that should be enough.

Have the strength, my own true love,
    to hear the truth Love speaks,
And know that His great purpose, dear,
    can't be finished in weeks.
Not in weeks, nor months, nor even years,
    can a perfect love be made,
But in the course of a loving life,
    complete Love can be had.

    Not easily, nor without some pain,
        for love starts rough and rude,
    But should we prick love 'cause of that pain,
        Love itself we would exclude.

Nor should we complain to the Potter, dear,
　　for what He strives to make,
For He sees far better than we do
　　and the course we ought to take.

And He sees our soul's strengths, my love,
　　and knows what we can stand,
And when He asks us for yet more,
　　He'll lend a helping hand.
And when He leads us into fire,
　　He knows quite well its feel,
He does it, dear, not to be mean,
　　but to make us tempered steel.

He'll give you the strength, my own true love,
　　to run to me today;
The distance may seem long and great,
　　but you will find your way.
You know the promised reason, dear,
　　why I can't come to you,
But do you see the other things
　　that our God's quite keen to do?

He wants, my love, to prove Himself
　　with these miracles for you:
Do you see your anger, dear,
　　and you disappointment too?
Those He can lift from off your heart;
　　easy 'nough for Him to do.
And do you see your fear and pride?
　　'Gainst Him they cannot last.
And the apparitions of your mind?
　　Those He'll banish to the past.

He will do this all, my love,
    if you'll only pray and ask.

Don't count the cost, my darling girl,
    for love is boundless deep,
And the more you give, my own true love,
    the more you'll find you keep.
Mere reason can't know all the costs,
    nor the priceless thing they buy,
So have the strength and faith, my dear,
    and straight to me please fly.

To let me hold you in my arms,
    as you hold me in thine,
To let Him hold me with your arms,
    as He holds you with mine.
This is our proper end, my love,
    to be well held by God above,
This is what He desires for us—
    to be made anew in Love Itself.

So run to Us now, Our prodigal girl,
    forget what the world might say,
Run to Us now, Our own true love,
    don't count what you must pay,
The things you'll lose are meager things,
    like pride, and fear, and doubt,
The things you'll gain are priceless things—
    they're what our soul's about.

Pride

It could have been a moment divine,
A moment in which you stepped beyond
    Your own self-imposed limitations,
And embraced your true potential.
You could have become who you were meant to be,
All that you were always meant to be,
Which is what my loving soul saw,
Filling my heart with pride.

It could have been a moment divine,
But in that moment you stepped back
    And remained right where you were,
Confined by your own self-embraced limitations,
Confined by your pride and fear.
You failed to be all that you could have been,
And filled my heart with sadness and disappointment.
Disappointment for myself…
    But sadness for you.

Jehanne

Once within a waking dream,
I had a vision true:
A young lass safe in my true love's arms,
A young lass I who I knew.

Now and then I've glimpsed her,
In times both good and bad,
A young lass as babe and child and girl,
A young lass happy and sad.

I've viewed her nurse at my true love's breast,
A small pink bundle of joy,
I've seen her toddle on shaky feet,
A ruddy lass of noise.

I've seen her run and I've seen her still,
Wide-eyed mischief on two feet,
And she's indeed her mother's child.
A beauty, smart and sweet,

A young lass named for a heroine,
A young lass named Jehanne.
Someday strong and reverent, and someday oh so bold,
For I've seen the dream to come.

Life's Song

Life is a song, beloved,
But then, of course, you already know that.

Why then do you stand mute?
Why then are you so afraid to sing?
Because those around you who do not know the secret will stare?
(Let them—perhaps then they too will learn to sing.)
Did I not show you the song that was yours to sing?
(Perhaps not, but then you never let me finish singing that song to
    you.)
Did you not recognize the song that was given to you?
(God's gift of grace wanted only acceptance,
Gratitude and love.)

Be not afraid, beloved.
Sing!

Sing out strong and saucy and with love.
Give up the comfortless, lukewarm existence you cling to
—It will not sustain you!
Release it—and release yourself from its bondage,
A suffering that was truly never meant to be.
Let your own true-self sing—Sing…
And give yourself to life's song.
Live!

"To live; that would be a great adventure."
It is a great adventure, beloved,
And it is never-ending…
When it is lived.

So be life itself, beloved…
Sing!

—*Isaiah* 61:1-2

The Magnificent Obsession

True love is a magnificent obsession,
The worth-shipful response when a pearl
    of great value is found,
When it is seen, when it is understood,
And when it is appreciated simply for what it is.
Love responds to its pearl, its beloved,
And to be worthy itself, freely gives itself away,
It gives itself as a free gift, but that is not enough.
And so it gives and must give not only itself,
But its whole heart, its whole soul, its whole being,
And everything it possesses as well.
Love thus consorts with its beloved
    more closely, more deeply,
And far more intimately than any other act of the soul.
So in love man dwells
    in value and worth and beauty itself,
Man becomes flowing goodness,
For goodness is the very breath of love.
In goodness, true love is the heart of fidelity,
And fidelity makes love visible and worthy
And utterly, perfectly real.

True love is thus not concerned
    with the beloved's station or position,
For those accouterments are trivial,
    poor cloth for the beloved.
Love is only concerned with its beloved's own true self,
With the beloved's very being.
And this it sees clearly, for before true love

The beloved stands naked and unclothed
    in the light of love.
Love thus sees its beloved clearly,
With a mystical, illuminated, crystal-clarity
In which every flaw and fault
    and short-falling are exposed...
And as quickly disposed,
For love sees the deeper beauty and responds.
Love steps beyond the imperfections of the beloved,
Non-characteristic blemishes transcended untouched,
For love sees the beloved as she is meant to be.
Love sees her own true self
And surrenders to the awe
    and mysterious wonder of it all.
True love is the magnificent obsession
    that disperses a good and loving soul
To its beloved and to the world,
Even as it gives the soul rebirth and satisfaction,
And makes it utterly, perfectly real and complete.

Masks

We all wear masks in this sad world,
And for a variety of reasons.
Some wear masks to hide from the world,
To hide their identity, good or bad,
From a world that would not understand or approve.
Some wear masks to hide from themselves,
To hide an identity, good or bad,
That they cannot understand or acknowledge or accept.

But someday, muirnin, you will take off your mask.
Someday you will look at it and see
    that the mask you wear is not who you are,
Or who you are meant to be.
Someday you will see
    that your cold, brass, worldly mask
Does not match your good, sweet soul
Or the warm, loving heart that the world is not worthy of.

Someday, muirnin, you will take off your mask.
And in that day you will finally allow
    yourself to simply be yourself—
Strong and bold and saucy; Passionate and loving,
Able to regard and disregard the world without fear,
And to finally make a scene and scenes;
The scenes God created you to make.

And in that day, muirnin,
    you'll see the mask you forced upon me.
But you'll know that I came to you
    respectfully unmasked
Unmasked in response to your beautiful prayer:

"O my dove…Let me see you, let me hear your voice,
For your voice is sweet, and you are lovely."
Then you'll know I opened my soul to you as to no other,
Rather than masquerading as someone else.

And then, perhaps, you'll finally understand
     why you couldn't accept
An unworldly Man without a mask of iron and clay.
You'll understand why you couldn't accept someone
Who loved unreasonably, yet wisely and well;
Why you couldn't accept
     a truth-telling rogue rebelling against the world,
Impetuous and bold and strong enough to wear no mask
In a world not worthy of us.

—*First Corinthians* 13

The Wizard's First Rule

Have you ever heard, dear,
Of the first of the wizard's rules?
It is a nasty fallacy, babe,
That plays us all for fools.

The fallacy knows we're rational, dear
And yet at the same time not,
It lives on our hopes and fears, babe,
And causes our reason to rot.

It shows us our heart's desires, dear,
And whispers those fancies are true,
It whispers that they're real, babe,
If only we really knew.

And it shows us our greatest fears, dear,
And whispers those fancies are real.
It whispers that they're real, babe,
'Til they're all that we can feel.

That rule it is quite strong, dear,
'Cause its words, not it, we feel.
It works on the heart of fancy, babe,
'Til only hopes or fears are real.

But those fancies are but apparitions,
Which we wrongly treat as real,
And give to our reason as fodder,
Thus our reason does it steal.

And with corrupted reason,
Our judgment's lost as well.

And with this corrupt judgment, babe,
Our happiness turns to hell.

Our perceptions get all twisted, dear,
And our reason gets the same.
Our judgment gets all mangled...
And we lose in sweet life's game.

—In appreciation to
  Terry Goodkind for his novel
  The Wizard's First Rule

Awe and Wonder

Philosophy begins in awe and wonder,
But a man's philosophy is his autobiography,
And my autobiography is filled with you.

I saw your face, your form, your external beauty,
But it did not move me.
I caught a glimpse of your mind and your thoughts,
And curiosity stirred me.
I looked closer.
I learned your beliefs, your loves, your dreams,
And you made me your friend.
I saw the goodness of your soul,
And the awe and wonder of it claimed me.

I looked at your face, your form, your quiet beauty again,
And now it moved me.
I looked at your mind and your thoughts,
And you pushed me to know
        my own intuitions and thoughts better,
To express my understanding of them more clearly.
I looked at you closer.
I examined your beliefs, your loves, your dreams,
And you made me know myself better,
I saw your soul in pure, crystal clarity, my own true self,
And the awe and wonder of you
        made me want to be a better man.

Love also begins in awe and wonder,
And a man's loves are his life,
So now my life is you.

The Best and the Worst

Look at man.
How great and terrible,
How small and pitiable,
An admixture of the best and the worst
That he could be or not be.

Alive, aware, and rational he,
Yet possessed by base desire.
Rational and yet irrational he,
But also sprung from a noble Sire,
Thus more—this man is free.

Free to think and free to love,
Free to doubt and fear;
Free to choose to doubt the truth,
Free to trust in lies;
Free to choose to be a fool,
Free to be quite wise.
Free to fear what is quite good,
Free to embrace what's not;
Free to choose to love the best,
Yet free to hate it too;
Thus free to choose to love the worst,
But free to spurn it too.

Look at this man, this paradox.
Aware, rational, and yet free,
An admixture of the best and the worst,
How small and pitiable he—
Yet how great and good he could be.

The Boat Rocker

We were not sent into this suffering world to be happy,
But to find out where our true happiness lies.
We were not sent into this poor world
    to be loved by men
But to find where our Love truly lies.

We were not sent to this suffering world
    to try to bring men joy,
But to show them where true happiness is found.
Yet we were sent to this poor world
    to give our love away,
And thus show men where Love can be found.

But we can't do that without rocking our poor boat,
We can't do that without breaking the calm.
We can't do that without rocking our poor little boat,
And causing its unhappy passengers some alarm.

Yet this is what we were always intended for—
We're not here to make things sweet and picture perfect,
We're not here to make things nice, or safe, or sound.
We're here to ruin ourselves, in a time of trial,
We're here to ruin ourselves for the sake of Love.

We're here to point to snowflakes
    and the perfect stars above,
We're here to point towards a higher end;
We're here to make a ruckus,
    we're here to cause a scene,
We're here to ruin self for the sake of Love,
By testifying to all men of God above.

We're here to live as adults, not content to live on pap,
We're here to eat real meat, meat red and rare.
We're here to lead a real live,
      our own, not someone else's,
And what their own ideas are,
      why, oh why, should we care?

And if they take exception, and rain out scorn and hate,
Why what more should truth expect than this?
For this has always has been the case,
      and it always will be so,
As long as our boat is captained by mere men.

As long as true Love doesn't rule,
      love must ruin all things,
As it must break our heart (but not our heart of hearts).
As long as this is so, love can only cause a mess,
And lead us to trial, tribulum, and death.
But far above the snowflakes,
      and far above the perfect stars,
There is a realm not ruled by men,
      a realm of peace and love,
Where we are not travelers, but its own true citizens.

—In appreciation to
J. P. Shanley and Nick Cage.
The first for his screenplay and
the second for his soliloquy in
Moonstruck

Crosses

In this poor world there are crosses for men,
And these crosses are made aplenty,
The mystery's knowing which to bear,
And which we were not meant for.

Some crosses are crafted by the world,
By men and false religions,
They'll wear a man down into the ground,
If these he tries to carry.
Step over this cross—the trick is not to lift it.

Some crosses are crafted by a man himself,
By his imagination or style,
They'll crush a man down into the ground,
If with one of these he tarries.
The trick is to put it down—Step past this cross

Yet Each man's given a true cross to bear,
A cross that will be a struggle,
But 'twill not crush him to the ground,
If he but knows the mysteries.

We cannot carry a man-made cross,
And our own true cross as well.
Two crosses are just too much weight.
They're more than one spirit can bear.

But we can carry our single cross,
If we know a trick or two.
We can carry our own true cross,
If we are but a few.

Help me carry my own true cross,
And with yours I will help you.
The paradox is, my own true friend,
One cross weighs more than two.

And as we cheer'y carry our load,
Another Friend will lend a hand.
One who's promised that as goes our day,
So'll go our strength as well.
Embrace this cross—the trick is to ask for help.

The Dance
(Both Ways Now)

"In the dance all idea of 'polite distance' disappears."

And you do want to dance, beloved,
More—you yearn to dance and to dance freely.
You yearn for a dancing partner
    to dance the dance of life with you,
More—you yearn for a partner
    who will flow smoothly with you,
Who will flow smoothly into you,
    becoming part of you.
More—Who will be you as much as you are you…
But too oft you want to keep him at a "polite distance,"
And that cannot be.

You want to know your dancing partner, beloved;
More—you yearn to know him intimately.
You yearn for a dancing partner
    to know the dance of life,
More—you yearn for a partner
    who will know you too,
Who will know your body and mind and soul,
    becoming part of you.
More—Who will understand you
    more than you understand yourself…
But you want to keep him at a "polite distance,"
And that cannot be.

You want to love your dancing partner, beloved;
More—you yearn to love him intimately.

You yearn for a dancing partner
    so you can love life's dance,
More—you yearn for a partner
    who will love dancing as you do,
Who will love dancing in the flesh and in the spirit,
    becoming part of you.
More—Who will dance within you
    as you yearn to dance within yourself…
But you need to keep him at a "polite distance,"
And that cannot be.

But though you yearn to dance, beloved,
More—you fear to dance in a world without dance.
And though you yearn to know a dancing partner,
    And yearn to be known in return,
More—you fear he'll learn your short-fallings,
    And the short-fallings you yourself will learn.
And though you yearn for a love,
    who through dancing,
Will become as much you as yourself.
More—You fear thusly of losing your self, dear,
But that's something that should not be.

You can't keep a dance partner at a distance,
Nor a knowing friend or your love.
You can't keep you at a distance from yourself,
    And be all you were meant to be.
You must open your arms, beloved,
    And embrace the dancer and the dance.
You must open your mind, beloved,
You'll find good outweighs bad not by chance.
You must open your soul, beloved,
And dance the dance of romance.

You must dance life's dance with rapture,
You must dance life's dance with trust,
You must dance not fearing the fall, dear,
For that's why your partner's so near.
You must pour yourself out to another,
If that partner is your own true self.
He'll see not a drop is spilt, dear;
That not a single drop is lost.
And he'll pour it all back with interest,
More—his love will make you anew.

Faith and Fear

"Now, what my love is, proof hath made you know;
And as my love is sized, my fear is so:
Where love is great, the littlest doubts are fear;
Where little fears grow great, great love grows there."

Now, as my love was proven,
    faith you should have known;
And as your love was equal sized,
    from fear you should have flown.
Yet I know that hist'ry hinders,
    and has birthed great fears in thee,
But as my love was proven,
    you should have faith'd in me.

Now, as my love was proven,
    faith you should have known;
And as my love was great, what I loved was even so:
A pearl of beauty rare, of goodness through and through,
But as my love was proven,
    you should have faith'd in you.

Now, as my love was proven,
    faith you should have known;
And as my love was Love itself,
    which also you've been shown,
You knew from whence our love came,
    from an Author of no fear,

And as His love's well proven,
    you should have faith'd in Him.

—The first stanza is from Shakespeare's *Hamlet*,
  Act III, Scene II, lines 166-169.

Faith and Reason

The sciences claim that they've no need of faith,
Observation and logic's the game.
What verifies best, is the trial and the test,
A caldron of data quite new,
Then sweet reason, it reaches into the mix
And plucks forth truths both beauteous and rare.

The truths it extracts are pure and exact,
Truths about stars and rocks…and 'bout men,
And the truths it extracts 'bout things living and dead,
There is no admixture in them.
For the truth science finds 'sa material kind,
The truth's matter is all that there is.

And if everything's matter, why would we need faith?
For free souls and God are no more.
Yet hid in plain view is a reason for faith
In the things 'pon which science depends.
Things like logic and reason, things for all seasons,
Surely science has faith in them.

Now religion it claims it does not need reason,
For faith is the name of its game.
Oh, reason does help, that can't be denied,
But in a purely subservient way,
For the great God above, speaks in glorious love,
And reveals truths we never could find.

The truths He reveals are sure and precise,
And quite beyond the science of men.
Truths about stars and truths about rocks,
And truths about God and men,

And the truths it extracts 'bout things living and dead,
There's always a mystery 'bout them.

There's a mystery 'bout stars and a mystery 'bout rocks,
There's a mystery 'bout all of creation.
There's a mystery 'bout freedom
    and a mystery 'bout men,
And a mystery 'bout God and 'bout dying.
But no mystery 'bout faith, for it's founded on reason,
And that reason's we heard what He said.

The Geas

A geas was laid upon me,
To see the world as it purely is.
A geas was laid upon me,
To speak truth as truth may be.

That geas was laid upon me,
When His gaze it turned to me,
That geis was laid upon me,
When His spirit came for me.

His geist laid it upon me,
He gave me a full life's task,
A task of work and duty true,
A job that lasts and lasts.

That geas sometimes feels like a curse,
When I'm taken for a fool.
Yea, that geas may be a curse,
When misunderstanding rules.

Yet it's also blessed me too,
For that geas shows me His trust,
And through it He stays near to me,
And through it brought me to you.

Now you're my geas, my own true self,
Who doubts and fears so well,
Now you're my geas, my own true self,
Who misunderstands oh so well.

A geas you are that's laid on me,
To see you as you are.

'Long with the geas to speak the truth
Of all the truths I see.

So I'm your geas as well, my love,
And thou' you're now confused,
You've had the intuition,
To see me as love's dove.

So I'm your geas, my own self true,
Thou' sometimes I'll be a curse,
Yet a blessing I will always be,
For this—I can put up with you.
(And love you every minute.)

—Author's note: I use the word "geas" or "geis" (prounounced 'gaze')
literally, to mean an obligation placed upon one by another, though
it is often used with the meaning 'a curse' as well.

Giving's Paradox

God does not say he loves those that bow,
Or pray long on calloused knee.
He does not say he loves the poor,
Or the suffering, or the meek.
But He says He loves the shepherd,
Who cares for his lost sheep.

God says he loves the giving hearts,
Who give of themselves with cheer.
He says he loves the souls poured out,
Who give in faith not fear.
He says He loves those blessed men,
And 'tis those whom He'll draw near.

Yet 'for He'll draw them back to Him,
He'll use them as His own.
They'll be his shining mirror here,
And be blessed where 'ere they roam.
And they'll be blessed still greater yet,
When He has drawn them home.

The paradox of giving then,
Is that those who give receive.
And those who freely give themselves,
Get back their every need.
The paradox of giving then,
Is that when all's poured out,

The joyful heart, the blessed noble,
Is now overfilled with God's own soul.

—*ἱλαρὸν γὰρ δότην ἀγαπᾷ ὁ Θεος.*
For the God loves the hilarious giver.
Second Corinthians 9:7

Grow Old Along With Me?

"Grow old along with me!
The best is yet to be,
The last of life, for which the first was made:
Our times are in His hand
Who saith, 'A whole I planned,
Youth shows but half; trust God: see all, nor be afraid!'"

What Browning's said's quite true,
These ancient truths I knew,
But now I see these words fall short as well:
The last of life was meant to last,
The whole's not meant to pass,
It's meant to dwell on, and on…and to dwell well.

And if youth shows only half,
So age shows only half,
Trust God: and then finally see the whole so sweet:
The end's not in growing old,
It lies in growing bold,
Accepting an eternal, child-like Being that's complete.

So grow young along with me!
The best truly is yet to be,
Eternal life, for which the temp'ral's made:
Our life is in His hand
Who saith, "A whole I planned,
Age shows but half; trust God: be child,
        and be not afraid!"

"So, take and use Thy work:
Amend what flaws may lurk,
What strain o' the stuff, what warpings past the aim!"

Our times be in Thy hand!

Perfect the whole You planned!

Let age approve of youth, and Life complete the same.

—In appreciation to
  Robert Browning,
  for his poem *Rabbi Ben Ezra*
  (*Grow Old Along With Me*)

Heroes

There is no hero without fear or doubt,
No heroism when the outcome's known
With no uncertainty.
There is no hero who acts without faith,
None who acts without paying a price,
That is, in some way, exacted with utter finality.

The real hero is imprisoned,
Enslaved to a cruel world of fact,
And those that understand that best,
Are those that suffer the most.
They are the ones who can be brought
To a great and near despair,
For when they learn of their frail selves,
They gain both anguish and pain.

The real hero is also imprisoned,
Enslaved to a cruel world of self,
And those that understand that best,
Are those that suffer worst.
For they are the ones who understand
That all choice resides in their hands,
And responsible for their own free selves,
They feel both anguish and pain.

Yet this great despair, this crisis of faith,
Is oft an act of Grace,
To those of true, bold spirit,
To those who understand,
To those who accept just who they are,

And thus dimly see the sustaining power
That's at their beck and call.

Every step of their life's journey,
Has brought them to this point,
A moment's revelation,
When they turn to face their fears,
When they cease to flee apparitions,
And demolish the lies they've birthed.

They see that fear that's run from it,
Follows throughout the night,
And as it follows, it just grows,
Gaining strength, and power, and might,
But they also see that fear long endured,
Fear that's both confronted and fought,
This fear is at least bearable,
For it's lost the power of its bite.

They see that these truths have value,
True virtues of their own,
And that their good, heroic acts
Are truths that bear virtue's name.
For these souls duty is the final test,
The test of the mettle and faith,
Which gives record of a new character,
And worthiness for a place of trust.

So they love these truths as well,
And become true heroes of faith:
Heroes like Abraham, the absurd,
And Isaac and the heel-catcher too.
Heroes like Joseph, the prophet,
And Moses who gave up all he knew.

Heroes like Joshua who tumbled the walls,
And Rahab, the harlot too.

Heroes that chose to be quenched in fire,
Rather than to be weak and flee.
Heroes that chose to walk into fire,
And count the world well lost for love.
Heroes that chose to be quenched in fire,
And pay whatever price t'was exacted,
Heroes that then walked through the great fire,
And emerged with the image and nature of God.

—In appreciation to
  Morris L. West, for his novel,
  The Shoes of the Fisherman

Michael Mann

The Hole in the Bottom of the Sea

God always was and always shall be,
    said the Theologian,
Or better yet, just simply say, "I am" is, and is, and is.
For God, says he, like the rolling sea,
    is infinite and indescribable,
Essence extending beyond all time,
    beyond the limits of his mind,
Beyond comprehension and nature.

I am, say I, like a rolling sea, infinite and indescribable,
Essence extending beyond time,
    beyond the limits of my own mind,
Beyond comprehension and nature.
And yet I see, I am less than He,
For there's a hole at the bottom of my sea.

There's a hole in my mind, and a hole in my heart,
There's a hole in the very soul of me.
There's a hole in the depths, in the deep abyss,
There's a hole at the bottom of my sea.

And though I am an infinite sea,
    that could ne'er pour through that hole,
And though that hole's in a deep abyss.
    so deep it has no bottom,
There's a more infinite Sea, far below me,
That "was" always there, calmly waiting to sustain me.

An infinite Sea, far below me,
    waiting to catch my soul's waters.
An infinite Sea, far above me,
    waiting to lift up my waters.

An infinite Sea, all around me, lifting my soul to His.
An infinite Sea, in communion with me…
    hard at work…
Closing the hole at the bottom of the sea.

Michael Mann

Horatio and Horatia

Horatia and Horatio,
As different as woman and man.
Horatio and Horatia,
As similar as summer and spring.

Horatia and Horatio,
One is just finding her roots.
Horatio and Horatia,
The other's grown strong
In the clefts of the rock.

Yet both are the self same person,
One soul that presents itself twice,
Full of strength and boldness,
Full of doubts and fright.

An odd mix of sure confidence,
Mingled with doubts sublime;
An odd mix of insecurity,
Mingled with faith in Him.

An odd mix of strong boldness,
And reason's sapping fears.
A saucy mix of passionate love
And fear's resplendent tears.

Yes, both lovers are the same,
For the summer once was the spring,
And what is now half grown
Once struggled to begin.

Yet one still trusts her own power,
Depends 'pon her own frail strength,

While the other's begun to tower
Having moved from strength to Strength.

One's faith is still a mustard seed,
Which has yet to reach its growth.
The other's a sprouting acorn,
That may someday be an oak.

Michael Mann

How Do I Love Thee?

How do I love thee, now that you are gone?
Let me count the ways your love has moved
    the depth and breadth and height of me.
Let me count the ways my soul is diminished
    when out of the sight of thee,
my own true love, the hint of Being, a gift of Grace.

I loved the passion of your endless kiss,
In most quiet need, and given by moon and soft starlight.
I loved the freedom given,
    after asked to follow you home by night;
I loved you purely, for I loved your purity…
    a purity I miss now.

Yes, I loved thee with the passion put to use,
But more than this I loved the more intimate touch,
The touch of mind on like mind,
Soul on like soul, which now is lost.

But most of all, my own true self,
    I loved thy very breath,
Your quiet, simple presence during my day,
The smiles, the tears, of all my life!—
And if God lets me pay the cost,
I shall love thee forever, and better after death.

—In appreciation to
  Elizabeth Barrett Browning
  for her poem *How do I love thee?*
  Let me count the ways

Humility

Humility, like love, sees reality as it is
And merely speaks the truth.
The man of humility sees truth,
And were there no God,
Would, in love, worship truth
For its inherent worth.

The man of humility, in love,
Merely speaks the truth.
He sees where he excels,
But does not merely acknowledge the fact.
He also praises God,
The God who leant him the talent to excel.

True, it is the man who's reason used those talents,
But the glory is still God's
For He gave the man the intellect as well.
True, it is the man who chooses to use those talents,
But the glory is still God's
For He gave the man free will too.
True, it is the man
     who had the strength to use those talents,
But the glory is still God's
For He gave the man that strength as well.

The man of humility, in love,
Merely speaks the truth.
And he sees where he falls short as well,
But does not merely acknowledge the fact.
He again praises God,
The God who leant him the talent

to see his own short-comings
And thus have the chance to change, to yet excel.

True, it is the man who's reason fell short,
But the glory is still God's
For He gave the man the intellect
    to see that he needs help.
True, it is the man who chooses to use his talents,
But the glory is still God's
For He gave the man free will
    to be seek one better than he.
True, it is the man
    who had the strength to use his talents,
But the glory is still God's
For He gave the man the strength to cry out for aid.

Invictus

Out of the night that covers me,
Black as the Pit from pole to pole.
I thank the Gods that surely be,
For my barely conquerable soul.

In fell clutch more than circumstance
I have oft winced and cried aloud.
Yet under bludgeonings not of chance
My head is bloody and gratefully bowed.

Beyond this place of wrath and tears
Looms more than Horror and the shade,
And thus the menace of the years
Finds, and shall find, me unafraid.

It matters not how straight my gait,
How charged with punishments the scroll,
I am the master of my fate:
I am the captain of my soul.

I've seen what's greater than the pole,
Greater than the Horror and the shade,
I've seen the Gods throw 'way the scroll,
And I alone could conquer my own soul.

Thus I mastered my own fate:
And truly captained my own soul,

I chose another 'for it was too late,
When I came to Love the Gods of old.

—With no apologies to William Ernest Henley
 (1849-1903), who was almost right.

The Keeper

In the dark, safe in my arms,
I've told you more than once,
You, ma coeur, my own true self,
Can't keep yourself from harm.

The best of women, that girl is you,
Of that I have no doubt,
Beauty, smarts, and charm w'out bound,
And a loving goodness too.

But you're just too prone to moodiness,
You're just too insecure,
Too prone to misunderstandings,
To find the way that's best.

You need a loving keeper, lamb,
To help you find the path;
Someone to help you when you lost,
And celebrate when you are found.

You know you need this keeper, dear,
You've told me with your smile,
You know you need a shepherd, girl,
And what you've sought, you'll find here.

Someone who'll guard your solitude,
Someone who'll be your strength,
Someone who'll love you for yourself,
Someone who'll watch over you.

Someone who'll push you when needs be,
To protect you from yourself,

And I too need the same thing, girl,
Someone who'll watch over me.

—For Ella Fitzgerald and Sarah Vaughn,
who sang "Someone Who'll Watch Over Me"
…so incredibly sweetly.

The Kiss

Your first kiss was a surprise, muirnin.
Not a brief brushing of lips, not a quick peck,
Not an instant's brief narrowing of the 'polite distance'
That separates two yet strangers
At the start of a dance that draws them
    into communion,
And union and oneness.

Your first kiss was a surprise, muirnin.
Not an instant's brief narrowing of the 'polite distance'
That separates two yet strangers,
But a dance of lips and arms and bodies
    that drew us into communion,
And union and oneness from the start;
A waltz that lasted…for a brief yet endless eternity.

Your first kiss took me flying, muirnin.
Your lips slipped the surly, weighty bonds
    of the earth from my soul,
    and made it light as a breath;
You flung it skyward with your lovely,
    silvered butterfly wings;
You sent me soaring heavenward,
    tumbling in mirth and joy,
Bathed in the radiance of a midnight sun
(When I could have sworn
    only the quiet, cold moon was present).
And high in the heavens you held me hov'ring there,
    in footless halls of air,
In wind-swept heights, and supported me
    with easy grace;

And you birthed in me a hundred desires and passions
    that I had only hoped to feel again.

Up, up the long, delirious, burning blue you sent me,
And with silent lifting mind and loving soul,
In the high untrespassed sanctity of space,
Lips upon lips, you allowed me
    to touch the face of God through you.

And when, at long last,
    that first, sweet, rich kiss drew to an end,
I fell earthward, out of control,
    almost shaking and breathless.
But you caught me in your gentle arms
And held me safe and warm.

And were that not enough of a miracle, muirnin,
Every kiss since then has done the same again.

Learn

I know that you are mature, beloved,
And insightful and bright and good.
But you are still young too, girl,
With much yet still to learn.

You need to learn to understand,
This first and above all:
How to work through misunderstandings,
Without losing it all.

You need to learn to understand,
How to fight without losing love.
You need to learn to understand,
How to set aside poor dignity.

And how to regain it in forgiveness.
But most of all there's this,
You need to learn to understand,
That you can trust yourself.
And your true intuitions.

Love

Love should be a comedy,
A thing of mirth and joy,
For we can't help but stumble,
O'er our limbs or tongues.
And if we can just laugh at those,
We'll always be amused.

Love should be empassioned,
A thing of worth true seen,
When we stumble o'er another,
And see our perfection there.
And if we both can reach out,
We'll always be well used.

Love should be a tragedy,
A thing of sorrowed pain,
For we can't help but fail, sometimes,
Causing hurt and fear.
But if we can just have some faith,
We'll ne'er give in to doubt.

Love should be a comfort,
In response to another's pain,
And if we try we'll help, sometimes,
And thrill at our other self's gain.
So if we can just give some love,
We'll know we've been well used.

For Love, it is a miracle,
A thing of wondrous awe.
Which despite stumbles and short-fallings,
Is what we were built for.

And if we can just see that,
We'll never quit, confused.

For Love, it is a miracle,
A thing of wondrous awe.
Which, despite the costs and sorrows,
Is what we were built for.
And if we can just pay those costs,
We'll get back more by far.

Love's Sight and Insight

Love, true love, it is not blind,
It sees what there is to see.
And more than this, it sees the beloved
As she was meant to be.

I saw your sweet disposition,
Your kind and caring ways,
Which sees mankind just as it is,
And cries for its poor souls.
I see also you moodiness,
That you sometimes must withdraw,
To find a little solitude,
And let your sufferin' self heal.
I know you know yourself some,
And know your heart is good,
Yet, I believe, I value more
That caring heart than you.

I saw your native intellect,
Your rational, probing mind,
Which tries to see things as they are
With logic and sense so fine.
I see also your feelings,
And your imaginations too,
And how they sometimes do intrude,
And deceive even you.
I know you know yourself some,
And know your mind is good,
Yet, I believe, I value more
That formidable mind than you.

I saw your natural goodness,
Your love of our great God,
And everything that He has made,
On earth and up above.
I see also how you sometimes
Care too much for what others think,
And thus forget 'bout mercy,
And even forget to forgive.
I know you know yourself some,
And know your soul is good,
Yet, I believe, I value more
That precious soul than you.

I saw your natural beauty,
So quiet and so refined,
A gentle beauty that will last
Until the end of time.
I see also imperfections,
A few, just here and there,
And how your beauty hides itself
When you scowl and when you frown.
I know you know yourself some,
And know you're pretty too,
Yet, I believe, I value more
Those exquisite looks than you.

I saw your strength of character,
A bold and saucy sort,
And I saw your budding faith
Which can pay whate'er it ought.
I see also your doubts and fears,
And your dread nightmares too,
I see how they sometimes delude,

And so you oft pay naught.
I know you know yourself some,
And you know your faith is true,
Yet, I believe, I trust you more
Than you can yet trust you.

I know this all, my own true-self,
For true love is not blind.
It sees true love as she's meant to be,
But more, much more I've found:
While true love sees its beloved
As she is meant to be,
True love also loves her,
Just as she is seen.

—In appreciation to
   Dietrich and Alice von Hildebrand
   for their book: *The Art of Living*

Lust?

When I told you of my dreams,
To lie with you as one;
To hold you close, to hold you near,
To hold you safe and warm;
When I told you of my dreams,
To love you as love must;
To tend you sacred garden, dear,
Why did you call it lust?

Did you not often ask me, love,
To follow you home at night?
Did you not hunger for love's words
With skittish, expectant might?
Did you not hunger for my lips,
To be held in comforting arms?
And to feel me trace your own sweet curves,
Knowing you were safe from harm?

Did you not often ask me, love,
To hold you through the night?
To kiss you neck and throat, dear,
With skittish, expectant might?
Did you not thus imprison me,
Within love's sweet embrace?
And hold me, love, throughout the dark,
'Til sunrise warmed my face?

Did you not give me freedom, love,
To trace your curves so sweet?
To feel the swelling of your breasts,
And cause our lips to meet?

Did you not take the freedom, love,
To kiss my throat and chest?
To place your trembling body close,
And in a single breath to meet?

Did you not also tell me, love,
Of your own wish to be one?
To give yourself without reserve,
To my Father's son?
Did you not desire the same as I,
For body and soul to mix?
For all our separate essences
Into one self be fixed?

So why then is your passion pure,
And mine just merely lust?
Why then is your soul noble gold,
And mine just clay and rust?
Do you not know where true Love burns,
Desire is Love's pure flame?
The language of our nobler heart,
Reflected in earthly frame?

—In appreciation to
  Samuel Taylor Coleridge,
  for his poem *Desire*

The Most Beautiful Things

"The most beautiful thing we can experience
    is the mysterious," he said.
And he was completely right.

When I was a boy, I stood in my front door,
And gazed at a sky so black, it rivaled the night
Until brilliant, blinding, crackling bolts
    illuminated the street
And the houses on it—until the rains came.
Rains so hard that the street and its homes
    were blotted from view,
Even when the lightning flashed,
Creating a whiteness and a wash of thunder
    that bathed me,
Even hidden away, safe inside the house.
The storm is mysterious,
And it is beautiful.

When I was a boy, I laid on my stomach in the grass,
And gazed at the fire flies winking
    yellow-green in the night,
Or sometimes glowing with a ruddy light,
And sometimes, rarely, occasionally
    with a pure, clean blue.
When I was a boy, I rolled over
    onto my back on the grass,
And gazed up at the distant fires
    twinkling crisp, clean and white in the night,
Or sometimes shining steadily with a cool ruddy light,
Or others burning hot and strong, blue and bright.

The fires near and far are mysterious,
And both are beautiful.

When I was a young man,
    I sat on a virgin green mountain-side,
And gazed at the sun as it retired in the west,
Shedding a ruddy light upon puffy, glowing clouds
Of salmon and yellow that brightened
    to gleaming scarlet and gold
Before fading into a dark, rich, royal purple.
Unlike MaGee, I did not reach out my hand
    and touch the face of God.
So God reached out and touched my heart
    and soul instead.
The sunset is mysterious,
But God is more mysterious yet.
And both are beautiful.

When I was a man, I sat with a loving lass,
And gazed at the light in her eyes as I held her close,
Marveling that she loved me in return,
A love that lasted year after year
    despite my faults and flaws.
When I was a man, I lay with that loving lass,
And later stood by her as she delivered to me
    the fruit of our love,
A babe so small and weak and needful,
But, oh, so perfect that it pulled at my heart
    as a sunset could not.
That lass is mysterious, and so is that babe,
But life is more mysterious yet.
And all are beautiful.

Years later, I sat with my loving lass,
And gazed at the light still sparkling in her eyes
    as I held her close,
Giving her what comfort I could
    as she was racked with a pain,
From a sickness that all the miracles
    of modern Aesculapians could not touch.
Little later, I sat with that same loving lass,
And watched the sparkle fade in her eyes,
Watched strong words and a bright mind
    fade into insensibility,
Watched her breath fade,
    leaving only stillness as it departed.
Death is mysterious.
And it can be beautiful too—
    for the Man who had touched my heart and soul
Had used death to heal my beautiful lass
    and then taken her home.

When I was older, I sat with another loving lass,
And gazed at the light in her eyes as I held her close,
Marveling at not just the love that she promised me,
But that she could see into my soul
    and shared my hopes and dreams and loves.
Yes, she could see into my soul
    and share my hopes and dreams and loves,
But she could not see into my mind
    to know the meaning of my poor words.
She could not see what she asked,
    or herself, or the source of her fears,
And misunderstanding me and herself, she fled.

That lass was and is a mystery,
worth spending a lifetime to know,
And my beloved is beautiful.

Now, even older still, I lay on my back in the cool grass,
The sunset has faded to black
and the fire flies have retired.
My children are grown and my other loves
are gone as well.
I am alone—and yet, I have learned,
I am never truly alone.
Overhead a riot of distant fires twinkle
crisp, and clean, and bright in the night.
And in its vault, at the heaven's zenith,
Swimming above the pale milky way,
Cygnus burns brightly,
Silently proclaiming that all His works are good.
And His works are good, works that include
all the blessings of life and love
That my Darling has given me day in and day out.
Works as mysterious as the loving gratitude
He fills my lonely heart with,
And this is beautiful too.

The most beautiful things we can experience
truly are mysterious, as he said.
And he was perfectly right.

Music

There is this about music,
There is always ever so much more to learn,
For however much we know,
There are ever so much more of song
That we do not yet know.

There is this about nature,
There is always ever so much more to learn,
For however much we know,
There is ever so much more
    'bout the music of the spheres
That we do not yet know.

There is this about reality,
There is always ever so much more to learn,
For however much we know,
There is ever so much more 'bout the song of being
That we do not yet know.

There is this about true Being,
There is always ever so much more to learn,
For however much we know,
There is ever so much more
    'bout the great Song of Songs
That we do not yet know.

Michael Mann

My Lady of Misunderstandings

Have you ever been with the single person in the world
    Who fills your heart with joy?
Have you ever been with anyone
    who fits that description?
Have I?

I have, my Lady of Misunderstandings,
My sad Lady who dwells in the vale of tears.
But that vale is a place never meant to be inhabited,
    But passed through.

So pass through it, My Lady.
Pass through it and you will find
        that single person in the world
        Who fills your heart with joy.
He is out there, Lady,
        and you will trip over him someday.
You will trip and fall,
That I promise you.

—In appreciation to
  Nora and Delia Ephron, Tom Hanks,
        and Dabney Coleman,
  for the movie, *You've Got Mail*,
  And Nikolaus Laszlo,
  for his novel, *The Shop Around The Corner*

Reason and Love

Which would you prefer, ma Coeur,
Cold reason or warm, sweet love?

There were reasons aplenty not to approach you,
There were reasons not to speak.
And after I drew near and spoke,
There were reasons to walk away.
For there are always reason aplenty,
Reasons to misunderstand and to doubt,
Reasons to lose faith; to not try, and to not fight;
Reasons to quit and to walk away.
And the best reason not approach you was you;
Was your worth in every possible way.

But the best reason to approach you,
Was that same worth as well;
A worth which demanded recognition,
And commanded me to speak and tell.
And after I did draw near you,
And after I spoke and told,
Respect for you blossomed
        and commanded me to love as well.

And now love finds it hard
To find reasons to walk away,
For there are precious few reasons strong enough
To overcome love that understands;
Understanding love, that defies doubt—
That love is the heart of faith.
And that faith makes love real and tangible,
And that love wills us to try and try.

That love that will risk all to fight
For a friend it values and respects.
That love that will fight for rare values,
Thus refusing to quit is a must.
That love must refuse to be denied
And walk quietly into the night.

Self-Righteousness and Dignity

I once said that you had troubles, dear,
Caused by pride and self-righteousness and fear.
I was wrong.

But I also spoke near the truth, dear,
Of pride, yea Horatia, and fear,
Of pride that preceded our fall, love,
But a pride from uncertainty and fear.
Fear of what others would think and say,
Then pride seeking a dignity not real,
A dignity that's self-centered alone,
But false dignity just isn't you.

For you were meant to be proud and strong, dear,
And bold and quite loving too.
But false dignity sapped your strength, girl,
And drained out your loving self too.
False dignity is too self-concerned, dear,
Though it looks to a world that cares not.
False dignity's too legalistic, dear,
But self-righteousness? No, I think not.

But true dignity, ah love, you have that,
Don't you see it, my darling, my own?
True dignity's founded on true value,
Not opinions of a world without love.
True dignity's founded on respect, dear,
And you command that respect, girl, and love,
Love founded on respect and worth, dear,
And all those you'll find is enough.

So love yourself for who you are, dear,
Not for who you're attempting to be.
Love yourself for your own quiet beauty,
For that's a pure gift of Eli.
Love yourself for your own solid thoughtfulness,
For that too is a pure gift of our God.
Love yourself for your own gentle goodness,
For that goodness means you're present to God.

Love yourself with a love other-centered,
For your choice to immerse self in Him.
Love yourself with a love other-centered,
Your real dignity's foundation's not slim.
Then have faith in yourself, O my darling,
With that faith be true to yourself, dear,
With that faith you'll be true to Him too,
With that faith you'll be true to all men.

Now see yourself as I see you, my poor dear,
See yourself as you were meant to be.
And you'll see that I am not much wrong.

—This above all: to thine ownself be true,
    And it must follow, as the night the day,
    Thou canst not then be false to any man.
    Shakespeare (*Hamlet*)

The Trinity

What would the greater miracle be,
That the Three are One;
Or that the Three don't disagree,
When all is said and done?

The God of old seems wrath 'n might,
Jealous of His own great power.
The Christ seems to give up His all,
Yet from Father does not cower.
And the Spirit seems but love itself,
Invisible, giving to us her power.

One seems to be ungiving,
One gives, but not to us,
One gives us out of loving,
But all unseen, how can I trust?

The Jews of old and Christians too,
Looked down on Greek deities.
And even Socrates was wise enough
To question, what's piety?
Thus Jews and Christians, Moslems too
Affirm God's a singularity.

A black hole I just can't fathom,
A God who's too simple a being.
How can I ever come to faith,
What's three in one to mean?

Saint Patrick tried to tell us,
On Ireland's dewy sod,
Using a three-leafed shamrock,

To 'splain about our God.
Three leaves, he said, yet still one,
But this answer fails to do the job.

It doesn't solve the mystery,
For all three leaves look quite the same.
But Father, Son, and Spirit don't,
And seem to share only a name.

And later theologians,
Affirmed this did not work.
And claimed it's but a mystery
Which from faith we should not shirk.
While we cannot understand, they said,
That all are One's a belief we must take.

But what would the greater miracle be,
That three different Beings are really One;
Or that these Three don't disagree,
When all is said and done?

Isn't it more mysterious,
That unlike the Grecian gods,
The Father, Son and Spirit,
To each other loudly nod,
And suborn themselves in a pure act of love,
Married into Oneness in heaven above?

Tunnel Vision

How oft do we focus on one thing,
And fail to see the others left to us?

How oft does one thing upset us,
Or trouble us, or vex us mightily?
One great thing perhaps…
Or maybe just one little thing.

One little thing is all it takes
To draw our attention to it,
To focus our attention,
So that we fail to see all else.

One little thing is all it takes
To blind us to the things that remain,
To blind us to the blessings left to us,
And to the good that we've been given.

One little thing is all that it takes
To blind us to the things
    that perhaps come with frustration,
To blind us to the blessings
    that perhaps comes with irritation,
And to the good that comes to us
    hand-in-hand with a little anguish.

How oft do we focus on that one thing,
And fail to see what remains for us?
How oft do we focus on that one thing,
And fail to appreciate the blessings
And the good that is still ours?

Understanding II

Why should we try to understand one another?
How can we understand someone else,
When we can't even understand ourself?

Perhaps it is only because that in one another,
In some special other, can we find ourself,
And finally and truly see who we are,
In the eyes of a friend, in that mirror.

Yes, in the mirror of my true friend's eyes
My true self was reflected to me,
And then I did see who I was in those eyes,
And who I truly was meant to be.

Worth

You had a choice, my little dove,
Who hides herself away.
You had a choice 'tween gift and giver,
But from the giver you did stray.
And when you fled from the giver, love,
The gift too you lost on that day.

You had a choice, my trembling dove,
Who hides herself away.
The choice of apparent safety,
Or real love for endless days.
But when you turned to safety, love,
Safety fled you that sad day.

You had a choice, my trembling dove,
Who still hides herself away.
The choice of cold, lonely dignity,
Or the choice of foolish love.
But when you chose from pride, dear,
You lost the priceless on that day.

You still have a choice, my little dove,
So don't hide yourself away.
Your dignity's of little worth,
Choose to play the fool today.
And when next a giver you find, love,
Choose the true gift on that day.

—For what is a man profited,
  If he shall gain the [approval of] the whole world,

And lose [himself] his own soul?
Matthew 16:26

Your Real Self

Our own true selves aren't found easily,
Or without spending sweat and blood,
But toil with me for just a while
And then perhaps we'll see—
Who is your own true self?

Are you someone who wants to be
All that you can possibly be?
Someone who wants to be yourself?
One who works for this excellence?
Or will you be someone else?

Are you someone who wants to be
The person you should be?
Someone whose promises are real,
Someone whose word is true?
Will you stick through thick and thin,
And be what you should be?
Or will you be someone else?

Are you someone who wants to be
The person you need to be?
Someone who wants to be a friend?
One who chooses an other self?
And will you stick through thick and thin,
And carry him when he falls?
Or will you be someone else?

Are you someone who wants to be
The person you must be?
Are you someone who seeks the truth,
Someone whose sight is keen?

Michael Mann

And when you find it, so you then,
Will let fine Truth command?
Or will you be someone else?

Discernment

You trust in prayer, my darling,
And in our God above,
You trust that He'll point out the way,
With His discerning love.

But you think it's a trying process,
And in truth it often is,
But God doesn't move in our own time,
The eternity He moves in is His.

To us it seems He's always late,
Or comes to us too soon,
But to Him He's always right on time,
Precisely at high noon.

Ne'er a moment early,
Ne'er a moment late,
Our God is always right on time,
He always keeps a date.

And he always answers every prayer,
Though sometimes he says "no",
And when he does, it is because,
The best is what he knows.

You think discernment's long and hard,
And, dear, that's often so,
But He sometimes acts in moments, love,
To tell us all we should know.

That is the way he dealt with me,
When He showed me a beautiful fate.

And, yes, I chose to seize it swift,
So that I'd not be late.

I needed not a minute more,
Than the moment in which sight came,
What more is needed than to see,
When sight's provided in God's name?

All I did was trust in Him,
And trust the gift He gave,
For isn't He faithful and true?
Should I not be the same?

But because my sight was given,
In a different manner than yours,
You seem to think that your way's right,
And mine's somehow impure.

You seem to think God's limited,
To your expected way,
And that no one can have another,
And be in his light today.

And you seem to think you know His will,
Though your answer is not mine,
And I'm sure you prayed both long and hard,
But did you hear His answer—
Or the answer from your fearful mind?

Since I've discerned one answer,
And you have another found,
One must be in error, girl,
And that one should not abound.

I've examined my sweet vision, girl,
Given 'for I fell for thee,
And thought the cost of trust is high,
It is from Eternity.

So what of your own discernment, girl?
Is it from a higher place?
Or might it be from somewhere nearer,
From fears that wear another's face?

This happens all too easily,
For our senses cry out loud,
And with imaginations, a noisy lot,
Something can be lost in the crowd.
So in the shouting match of our minds,
God's polite voice, so soft and small,
May not be heard at all.

—For the God is not the author of confusion [instability],
  But of peace, as in all the churches of the saints.
  First Corinthians 14:33

The Valued

States of Affairs.
How many meanings can be contained
    in that simple phrase?

What is our "state of affairs"?
Are we having an affair, muirnin?
Not that the world would judge,
    though perhaps a prelude to one in its eyes
    for it sees intimacy in only one, raw way.
But that we are already deep in an affair de Coeur,
    an undeniably intimate affair seems a fact.
We both have the same feelings
    to the other's lips on our own,
    now gentle and probing,
    now insistent and demanding;
The same feelings to the other's arms around us,
    holding us safe and warm.
And perhaps more…certainly more
    when it comes to the intimacy of minds and souls
    that call so deeply to each other,
    more so than bodies do or could ever do.

This is a good state of affairs, muirnin.
Especially when you are in my arms,
    dressed in a certain little black dress,
    with a hint of pure white trim.
But that is not the state of affairs
    that insinuates itself into my mind,
    when, with loving hands,
    I trace the curve of your back,
    And when I now encounter

the zipper of that little black dress.
Then I could wish that our state of affairs
    was such that I could slowly slip
    the zipper of that little dress down
    and caress your naked back,
    flesh upon flesh to mirror lips upon lips,
    but then…
    I would not have wished to stop.

But our present state of affairs, muirnin,
    would have made that merely an affair
    and not the best state of affairs.
And what I desire is that beautiful state,
    that perfected state, in which we are wholly one.
True, sometimes, in that perfect state
    we would be wholly one, and one in the flesh,
    lips hard pressed and arms entwined,
    naked bodies—
    yet bodies that were not naked,
    but rather the joyously clothing
    our other self's body and soul.
But such intimacy is just the cherry,
    and other kisses and caresses
    and hugs are just the whipped cream.
The real substance of intimacy is the sundae,
    And life through the rest of the week as well.
The real substance is the "mere" shear presence
    of our other soul in life—
    and that, my darling muirnin,
    that is what we do now lack.

The presence of being together,
    the presence of being parted—

and never parted:
together even when in different rooms
or buildings, even those a world apart.
The presence in doing those little things
that speak of the love in one's own heart:
The intimacy of bringing you a single red rose,
For no reason other than love.
The intimacy of cooking you a simple meal,
or guarding your solitude;
The intimacy of supporting you as you work,
and bringing you chocolate or tea.
The intimacy of watching over you when you work,
without disturbing thee.
And the intimacy of spooning when our work is done;
and of rubbing your neck and back,
until your breathe becomes quite deep—
then as you breathe so gentle and slow,
the intimate thrill of your presence,
even as you sleep.

That is the best state of affairs, my love,
To share the gift of one's whole life
with a wholly intimate other.

Vision and Concern

If my vision was self-centered,
All I would see is me,
And all other things of beauty and worth,
I'd be too blind to see—
My only concern would be myself,
How poor then would I be?

If my vision was man-centered,
All I'd see would be reasoning men,
And all other things of beauty and worth,
I'd be too blind to see—
I'd be too concerned with what they thought,
And too unconcerned with Thee.

But if my vision is God-centered,
I'll see Him and all else,
For He sees the things of beauty and worth,
And recommends them all to me—
He sees all of nature's beauty,
Placed in my hands in trust,
So care for it, in duty to Him,
That becomes a must.

If my vision is God-centered,
I'll see Him and all else,
For He sees the things of beauty and worth,
And recommends them all to me—
He sees all of man's great beauty,
For in truth He made them all,

So to care for them, in duty to Him,
Is a duty that to me falls.

If my vision is God-centered,
I'll see Him and all else,
For He sees special things of beauty and worth,
And recommended them 'specially to me—
He sees the beauty of special friends,
And the beauty of you too,
So to love them is engraved in my heart,
Something for Love's sake I must do.

And if my vision is God-centered,
I'll see Him and all else,
And He sees the greatest beauty and worth,
And recommends Himself to me—
I see the beauty of our God,
And His wisdom, and love, and faith,
And from the Love engraved in my heart,
The choice to return love for Love,
Is a choice I freely make.

Family

Cold February became colder still,
    when my dear wife died,
My love for almost thirty years,
    my partner, still my bride,
The woman who knew me so well,
Lost her battle to her foe.

On this day all things changed,
    my home became just a house,
For on this day it lost its heart,
    its soul, its very life.
On this day my whole became a half,
And feared what was left of life.

I'd like to say what I learned next,
    but my words are to poor,
So let me use another's words,
    for nothing's needed more:

    "Losing family obliges us to find our family;
    Not always the family that is our blood,
    But the family that can become our blood.
    And should we have the wisdom,
    To open our door to this new family,
    We will find the wishes we once had…"

We will find the dreams we once had,
    the love we once had,
And our heart, once dead, will be returned to life.

    "[And should we not,]
    the only thing left to say will be,

'I wish I had seen this,'
Or 'I wish I had done that,'
Or 'I wish…'"

But then our hearts will be worse than dead,
For not another, not fell circumstance,
But our own fears will have made them only stone.

"Someone I once knew wrote…
We walk away from our dreams
    afraid that we may fail,
Or worse yet, afraid we may succeed."

Yet this also I've learned:
The things that gnaw most on one's soul,
    are not the thing's we've done,
They are not the things we've failed at,
But those things we've never tried,
The precious dreams and wishes we denied.

—In appreciation to
  Gus Van Sant, Sean Connery and Rob Brown for
  Finding Forrester

But You Know...

I know you think you know who you are,
And who you think I am.
But you are both wrong...and yet right too.

You know you're strong, and bold, and saucy,
And you are right and yet still wrong.
Strong and bold and saucy is who you're meant to be.
And who you are right now
      in your heart of hearts and your soul of souls.
But it is not who reason now allows you to freely be.
And so it's not who you are or who you pretend to be.
That is too little, girl, much too little for you—
So be all that you can truly be,
Just be yourself, beloved—
That's more than enough for God and me...
And should be enough to satisfy thee.

You think you know who I am,
A fool or cur or the like;
A disrespectful, pretentious snob,
And you are right and yet still wrong.
To the world I am each of those things,
But you know who I really am—
No more, but also no less than this,
I am who He made me,
      That's all I am:
I'm just an impoverished peasant,
      Yet birthed by high Royalty.
I am just a simple nobleman,
      Who tilts at windmills of steel.

I am just a simple soldier,
        In a long, well hidden war.
But I am a simple poet too,
Speaking the truths of Love.

And someday, baby, when you've grown,
When you finally spread wings true,
When you straighten up and fly right,
And see what you always knew,
Then find me, lady, on that day,
And claim a friend's hug, long delayed.

0-595-33970-0

Printed in the United States
63063LVS00003B/239

9 780595 339709